THIS BOOK BELONGS
TO

....................................................

Best Wishes

*[signature]*

First published in the United States of America in 2005 by
Rizzoli International Publications, Inc.
300 Park Avenue South
New York, NY 10010
www.rizzoliusa.com

Text copyright © 2004 Lulu Guinness
Illustrations copyright © 2004 Martin Welch
Design by the Simultaneous Workshop
Production Director: Anet Sirna-Bruder
Edited by Eva Prinz

Printed in Mexico
2005 2006 2007 2008 2009 2010 / 10 9 8 7 6 5 4 3 2 1
Library of Congress Control Number: 2004096826
ISBN: 0-8478-2694-5

# PUT ON YOUR PEARLS, GIRLS!

# Put On Your Pearls, Girls!

BY
## LULU GUINNESS

FOREWORD BY
HELENA BONHAM CARTER

ILLUSTRATIONS BY
MARTIN WELCH

RIZZOLI

# FOREWORD

ONCE UPON A TIME, three Christmases ago, my father asked me to buy a present for myself. I needed a handbag, a special handbag—always a tricky purchase. We are talking long-term relationships here. So I made a beeline for the shop of the Goddess of Handbags and it was there where I found the bag that has been at the end of my arm ever since. It is black with patent handles and bears a silhouette of the aforementioned goddess wearing a pearl necklace and her initials embroidered in white, along with the phrase "Put on Your Pearls, Girls." It is somewhat battered now, the bottom has begun to bow and sag but it still holds my mini life, the essential baggage I carry with me everywhere; and to me it is still beautiful. Like all happy pieces of design, it is a blend of the functional with the visually delighting. It has also proved to be a social asset, prompting smiles, conversation, and envy (the sign of a successful purchase) from strangers in queues, airports, Starbucks, and on streets and in shops across the world.

The Lulu you will meet in this book, dear reader, is not, I'm happy to say, a dictator. And this is why I prefer her and would refer to her as a style agony aunt over others. She is a champion of the individual whereas others want us all to copy and conform. Indeed, as far as I see it, the underlying and governing fulcrum of an idea upon which the whole of fashion is poised is that we should all look the same, i.e. we should all be sheep when, in fact, we were never meant to be clones. She is a defender of the rebel, a liberator of the inner girl, and *femme fatale*, or fun fatale. A confidence-giver and one who urges us to perceive our difference as uniqueness and to show it off, not hide it away. Looking at her style suggestions I see that unconsciously I have been observing the whole lot of them all my life. And I have definitely observed Elsa Schiaparelli's Fifth Commandment, as I would not be beyond wearing a shoe as a hat. Maybe Lulu's one suggestion I haven't lived by is Number Seven, as I have often dressed like a five-year-old, especially when my inner girl gets a bit too enthusiastically outer. Anyhow, I've never been one to grow up fast.

But then I suspect this is exactly what Lulu, and particularly this book, is about. It's a picture book, a pop-up book for us not-so-grown-up girls. She appeals to the five-year-old girlie in all of us; exhorting us to wear our inner girls on the outside. I have always loved her aesthetic, her wit and whimsy. Her world into which she invites us to step, or skip, is one where we can dream and fantasize, regress and dress up in our Mum's clothes; walk back to the '50s and borrow from our mothers, when women were fabulously feminine and decorative and flirty and pretty. But unlike our forbears we do it because we choose to, not because we don't have any other option. In Le Monde de Lulu we can have our cake and stuff ourselves, and then, if we're fat, as Lulu says, "shop for accessories."

This book, dear reader, is like all of Lulu's creations: a delicious confection, a little life-enhancer. Lulu in turn observes one of my own little aspirational aims in life, which is to remember to live with imagination; to bring fantasy to the quotidian; to splash what can sometimes be the gray and drab days with a little pink. So if you are in need of a touch of pink just take your fingers for a walk in this book. I hope it enchants and that it lands on the top of your bedside tower. And if, unlike me, you have a little girl, I suspect the author might approve of it being read by both mother and daughter simultaneously. A little bedtime style instruction.

And finally, as I write this, Christmas has come around again. My father is no longer with us, but I carry his bag around with me wherever I go. Quite serendipitously, the other big man in my life, Tim, gave me a string of beautiful, very real pearls that hang around my neck and which have not left it since I was presented with them three days ago on Christmas Eve. I have written these words in them. I have truly fulfilled Lulu's and Dad's commandment. And I have yet to tell Lulu that even though he's not a girl, my son Billy loves wearing them, too (much to his father's slight consternation). But then he is our oyster boy.

HELENA BONHAM CARTER
LONDON, 2005

Poised

Elegant

Attractive

Radiant

Ladylike

Sophisticated

# INTRODUCTION & ACKNOWLEDGMENTS

LULU IS A fictional character, based on myself, except that she is timeless, ageless, and has long legs I can only dream of possessing. Through her I am trying to encourage you to live life with wit and wisdom, and to find the confidence to create an individual style for yourself on the outside and—perhaps most important of all—to have a good heart on the inside. *Put On Your Pearls, Girls* is meant to inspire you to be proud of your femininity and to laugh at yourself and with others. I could not have created "Lulu" or the world that she inhabits without the great talent of Martin Welch, my illustrator. He shares my sense of humor and a passion for the work of great fashion illustrators, such as Grau, Warhol, and Cocteau, to whom we pay homage in this book. *Put On Your Pearls, Girls* is very personal to me. I hope it will surprise you, inspire you, and bring a smile to your face.

I would like to thank Charles Miers, my publisher, who has for several years encouraged me to write my book and who went beyond the call of duty to make sure it happened; Eva Prinz and Andrew Prinz at Rizzoli for giving so much of themselves to this book; and Tara Sharpe of Lulu Guinness Ltd., without whom this book would never have been completed. Very, very special thank yous to my daughters, Tara and Maddie, who put up with me being away so much; to Julianne Smith—there's no way I could do it all without you; and to Valentine Guinness, for being such a good father. Last, but not least, I thank the college girls who told me that when they need encouragement they have a phrase, borrowed from one of my handbags; they text message each other: "Put on Your Pearls, Girls!" When they told me that, I knew I had a title, and a message, to connect with all ages.

*Lulu Guinness*

LULU GUINNESS
LONDON, 2005

Introducing Lulu!

Lulu is not a Morning Person...

Some days you wake up...

On Top Of The World!

Other days you feel...

FRAGILE HANDLE WITH CARE

LONDON

DRESS TO SUIT YOUR MOOD!
Don't Keep All Your Most Glamorous Things
for Special Occasions.

Follow
Elsa Schiaparelli's
5TH
Commandment:

90% are afraid of
Being Conspicuous, and of
What People Say.
They should
Dare To be Different!

Why Don't You Wear a Cocktail Dress To The Office?

If You Want To be Drop Dead Gorgeous,
Why not be a Hitchcock Heroine
For the Day?

Put
On
Your
Killer
Heels!

But
Don't
Forget...

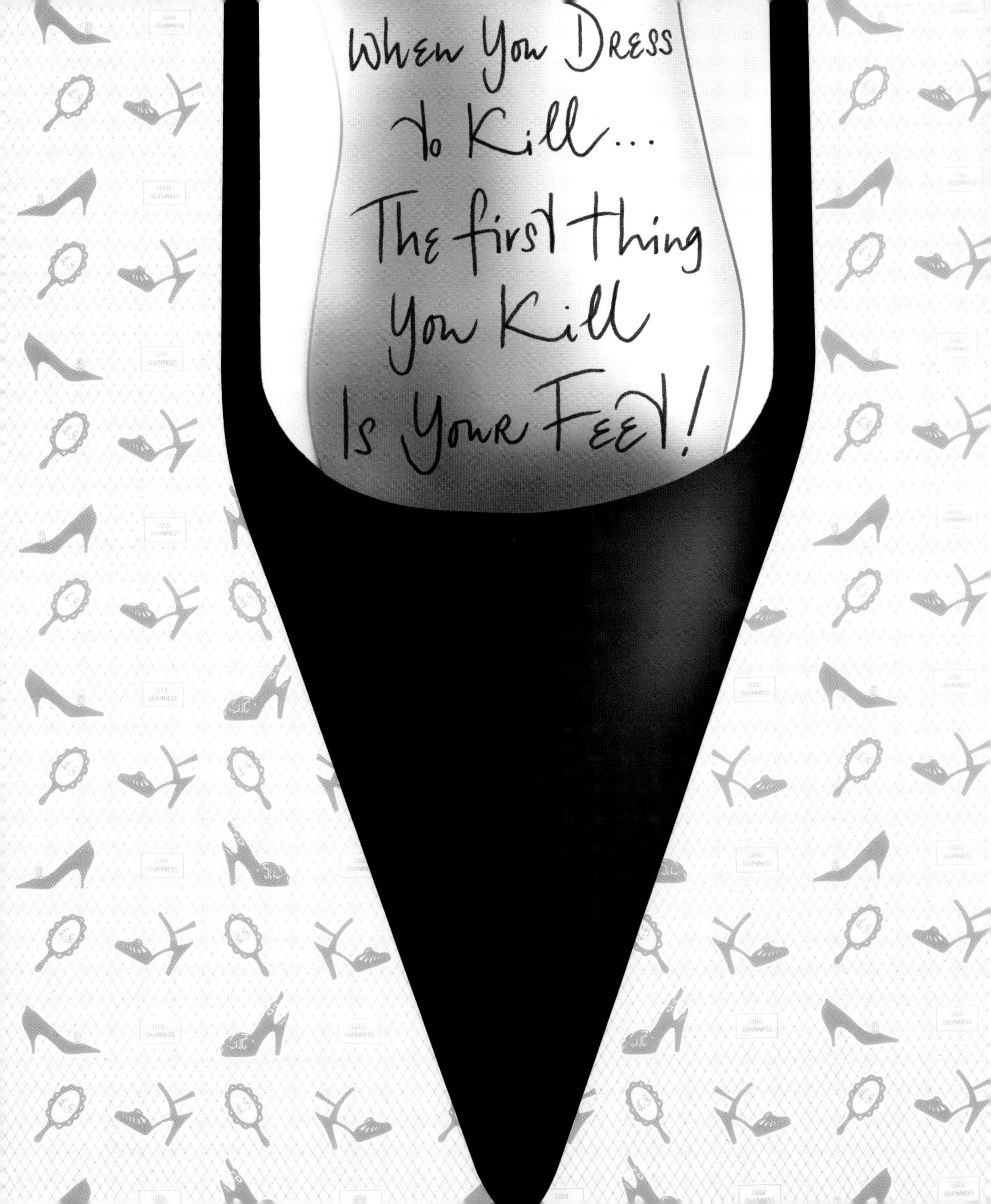
When You Dress
To Kill...
The first thing
You Kill
Is Your Feet!

Powder Your Nose...

∞ Lulu's 12 Suggestions for Women∞

1. Create a style that is uniquely yours—
   Don't be a slave to fashion.

2. Money does not equal style.

3. Mix vintage with modern—couture with chainstore.

4. If you're feeling fat—why not shop
   for accessories?

5. Carry bags of personality.

6. Never take fashion or yourself too
   seriously.

7. Mutton dressed as lamb is NEVER a good idea.

8. Less can be more – but sometimes MORE is MORE.

9. Beauty comes from The heart – Not from a jar.

10. You CAN be Too Rich or Too Thin.

11. Be who you WERE meant To be – NOT who others Think you ought To be.

12. Put On Your Pearls Girls!

While Window Shopping is good

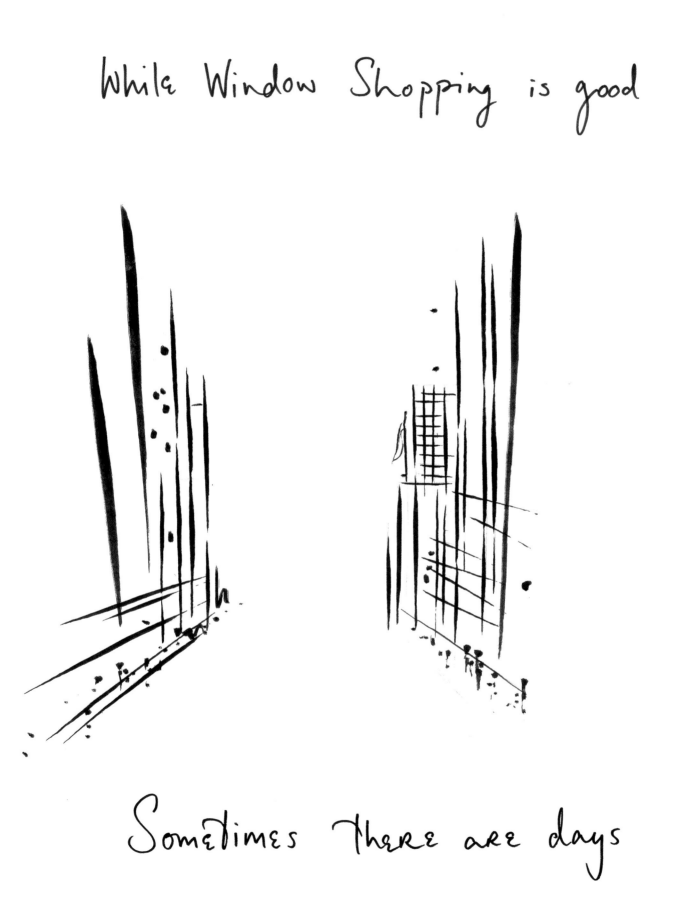

Sometimes there are days

...Shop Till You Drop!

And then there are days when

Only chocolate will hit the spot

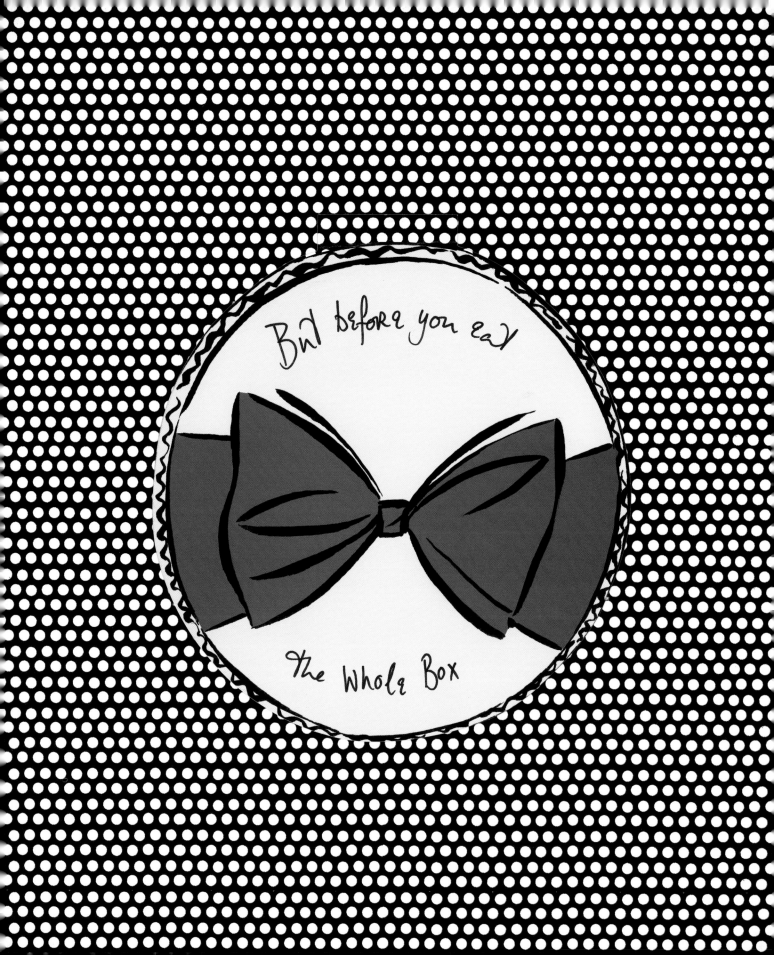

CREATIVITY
BEGINS
AT
HOME

*From window Box....*

To Grand Estate,

Gardeing is Good for the Soul.

To Grand EsVale,

Gardeing is Good for the Soul.

There's another world

inside your head.

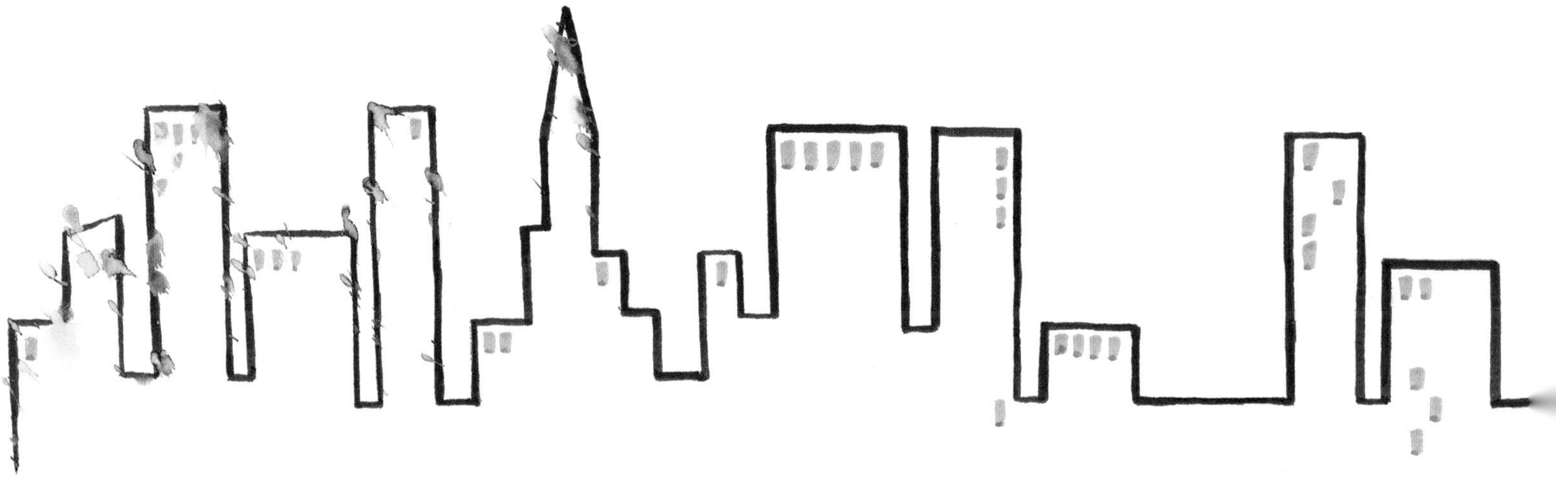

Use Your Imagination,

Trust Your Instinct,

and Follow Your Dreams...

But Be Careful What You Wish For!

is The Best Accessory.

Just Remember—

You Don't have To be

The Life a Soul of The Party

Every Night!!

NEVER BE THE LAST

*To Leave a Party....*

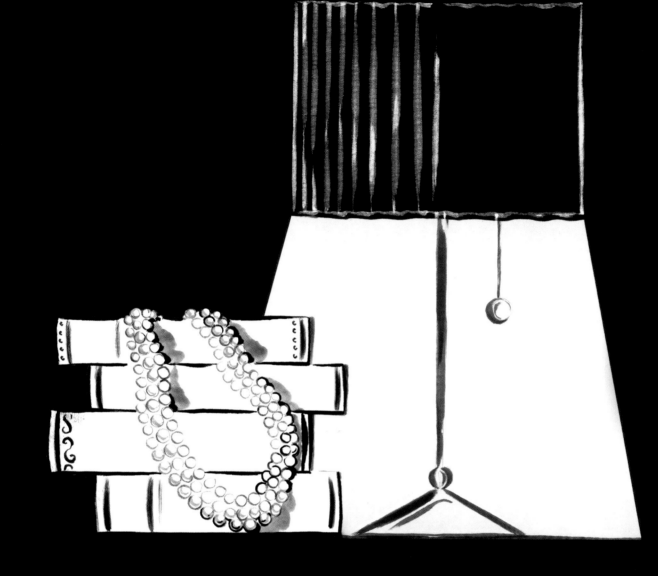

Before Going To Sleep

Count Your Blessings

*The End*